POSITIVE
Affirmation
Prayer Book

ISBN 979-8-88616-336-0 (paperback)
ISBN 979-8-88616-337-7 (digital)

Christian Faith Publishing
832 Park Avenue
Meadville, PA 16335
www.christianfaithpublishing.com

Printed in the United States of America

POSITIVE
Affirmation
Prayer Book

Affirmation and Prayers to Comfort and
Bless You throughout the Day as You
Meditate the Wonderful Messages of God

Raluca Boyle

Calm Affirmation

I foster calm energy in my mind, body, and spirit.

Create in me a clean heart,
O God. Renew a right spirit
within me. (Psalm 51:10 KJV)

Happiness Affirmation

I am happy and content with my life.

Commit to the Lord whatever you do, and he will establish your plans. (Proverbs 16:3 NIV)

Shielding Prayer

Dearest angels, please surround and protect me with a bubble of light today. Shield my energy from all negative influences. Showering healing white light over me, help me to keep my energy pure, clean, and in high frequency.

Arise, shine, for thy light is come, and the glory of the Lord is risen upon thee. (Isaiah 60:1)

Anxiety Affirmation

I'm in charge of my mind and body. I am capable of solving any problems that face me.

Do not be anxious about anything. But in every situation, by prayer and petition, with thanksgiving, present your requests to God. (Philippians 4:6 NIV)

Fearlessness Affirmation

My fears will not stand in the way of my goals. I let go of fearing mistakes and failure. Each day I become more and more brave. I have nothing to be afraid of. I am brave!

9

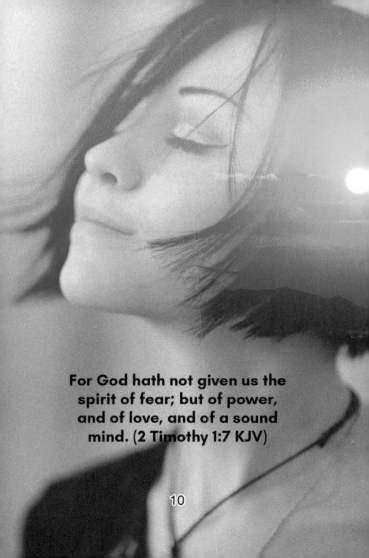

For God hath not given us the spirit of fear; but of power, and of love, and of a sound mind. (2 Timothy 1:7 KJV)

Cleansing Prayer

May I release all energies that are less than love and free my mind and body of all that no longer serves me. I send back any energies that are not mine, with love. I anchor into myself the present moment.

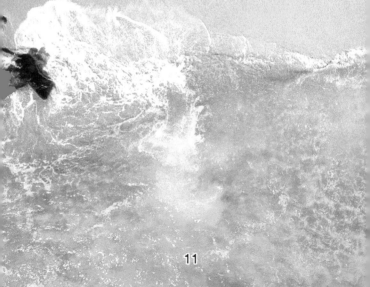

Now may the God of peace himself sanctify you completely and may your whole spirit and soul and body be kept blameless at the coming of our Lord Jesus Christ. (1 Thessalonians 5:23 KJV)

Christ Wholeness Affirmation

I am God's perfection manifest in body, mind, and soul. I trust that God is guiding my path to keep me whole!

And with that he breathed on them and said, "Receive the Holy Spirit." (John 20:22 NIV)

Abundance Affirmation

I now allow myself to have more than I ever dreamt possible.

The Lord loves the just and will not forsake his faithful one. (Psalm 37:28 KJV)

Angelic Guidance Affirmation

I am a pure, radiant being filled with love and light. I am divine intelligence, I am one in the heart of universal love, I am the love of God, I am wrapped in the loving energy of the archangels, I am the love of heaven, and I am the love of my higher self. I am open to the advice of my guardian angels. Angelic guidance is given to me constantly. I am here to awaken the potential and wisdom of my soul.

For the Son of man shall come in the glory of his Father with his angels; and then he shall reward every man according to his works. (Mathew 16:27 KJV)

Peace Affirmation

I now release and send all
negative energy to the light.

But they that wait upon the Lᴏʀᴅ shall renew their strength; they shall mount up with wings as eagles; they shall run, and not be weary; and they shall walk, and not faint. (Isaiah 40:31 KJV)

Courage Affirmation

I am courageous, fearless,
and bold in all that I do.

I can do all things through Christ who strengthens me. (Philippians 4:13 NIV)

Trust Affirmation

Everything is happening perfectly
in my life. The universe naturally
takes care of me and my needs.
I am completely aligned with the
universe. I trust that everything
happens for a reason.

The Lord is near to all who call
on him, to all who call on him
in truth. (Psalm 145:18 NIV)

Purpose Affirmation

All that I need is drawn to me.
I can achieve greatness.

My God will meet all your needs according to his glorious riches in Christ Jesus. (Philippians 4:19 NIV)

Victory Prayer

Lord, I thank you for the victory.
You are my Savior and King. You
have fought my battles for me
and made me victorious in you.
Because of you, I never have to
know eternal death, and I will be
safe from the snares of hell. Amen.

But thanks be to God, which giveth us the victory through our Lord Jesus Christ. (1 Corinthians 15:57 KJV)

Purpose Affirmation

I attract lucrative, enjoyable, and beneficial circumstances.

And we know that all things
work together for good
to them that love God, to
them who are the called
according to his purpose.
(Romans 8:28 KJV)

Focus Affirmation

I am capable of accomplishing
my tasks and responsibilities. I
am focused and disciplined.

And to knowledge, self-control; and to self-control, perseverance; and to perseverance, godliness. (2 Peter 1:6 NIV)

Calm Affirmation

I allow tranquil and serene energy, thoughts, and things to flow easily to me.

But when you ask, you must believe and not doubt, because the one doubts is like a wave in the sea, blown and tossed by the wind. (James 1:6 NIV)

Confidence Affirmation

**I believe in myself and my abilities.
My potential to succeed is limitless.**

Now this is the confidence that we have in Him, that if we ask anything according to His will, He hears us. (1 John 5:14 NKJV)

Strength Affirmation

I am already in possession of the strength required to triumph over doubt and fear and achieve excellence, in every area of my life.

Yea, though I walk through the valley of the shadow of death, I will fear no evil: for thou art with me; thy rod and thy staff they comfort me. (Psalm 23:4 KJV)

38

Healing Affirmation

I allow peaceful and healing white light to flow through my body now.

Heal me, O Lord, and I will be healed; save me and I will be saved, for you are the one I praise. (Jeremiah 17:14 NIV)

40

Power Affirmation

I am a powerful being who can do anything I put my mind to. I am always striving to be the best version of myself.

Trust in the Lord with all your heart: and lean not unto your own understanding. In all your ways, acknowledge Him, and he will direct your paths. (Proverbs 3:5–6 NKJV)

The Lord's Prayer

Our Father which art in heaven, Hallowed be thy name. Thy kingdom come, Thy will be done in earth, as it is in heaven. Give us this day our daily bread. And forgive us our debts, as we forgive our debtors. And lead us not into temptation, but deliver us from evil: For thine is the kingdom, and the power, and the glory, for ever. Amen. (Matthew 6:9–13 KJV)

For the LORD is good; his mercy is everlasting; and his truth endureth to all generations. (Psalm 100:5 KJV)

Protection Affirmation

I am divinely guided and
protected at all times.

Ask, and it shall be given you; seek, and ye shall find; knock, and it shall be opened unto you. (Matthew 7:7 KJV)

Addiction Affirmation

I am mentally strong enough
to let go of any addictions or
habits that do not serve me.

Because he himself suffered
when he was tempted
he is able to help those
who are being tempted.
(Hebrews 2:18 NIV)

Love Affirmation

Life is very simple. What I give out comes back to me. Today, I choose to give love.

Those who plan what is good
find love and faithfulness.
(Proverbs 14:22 ESV)

Gratitude Affirmation

I am grateful for my health, family, friends, success, and other blessings. I gratefully accept more of it each day.

In every thing give thanks:
for this is the will of God in
Christ Jesus concerning you.
(1 Thessalonians 5:18 KJV)

Self-Confidence Affirmation

I can make positive connections with other people around me and feel confident and at ease being myself.

Grace be with you, mercy, and peace, from God the Father, and from the Lord Jesus Christ, the Son of the Father, in truth and love. (2 John 1:3 KJV)

Focus Affirmation

My mind is clear and focused. I have
a vision, and I work for it every day.

And do not be conformed to this world. But be transformed by the renewing of your mind, that you may prove what is that good and acceptable and perfect will of God. (Romans 12:2 NKJV)

Wellness Affirmation

I let go of upsetting energy and embrace peaceful energy in its place. I am spiritually strong.

For we wrestle not against flesh and blood, but against principalities, against powers, against the rulers of the darkness of this world, against spiritual wickedness in high places. (Ephesians 6:12 KJV)

Wealth Affirmation

**Money flows to me in expected
and unexpected ways.**

For I know the plans I have for you, declares the Lord, plans to prosper you and not to harm you plans to give you hope and a future. (Jeremiah 29:11 NIV)

Gratitude Affirmation

I am grateful for this wonderful day. I am grateful for all that I have and all that is coming to me.

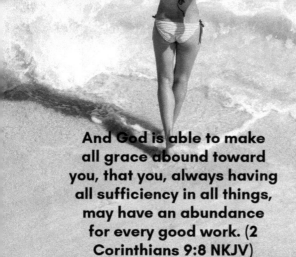

And God is able to make
all grace abound toward
you, that you, always having
all sufficiency in all things,
may have an abundance
for every good work. (2
Corinthians 9:8 NKJV)

Crown Chakra Affirmation

I am connected with my higher self and the divine sprit for positive energy. I am at peace, guided by my inner wisdom.

In God is my salvation and my glory, the rock of my strength, and my refuge, is in God. (Psalm 62:7 KJV)

64

Third Eye Chakra Affirmation

I am open to my intuitive abilities
and use them for my highest good.

Now unto him that is able to do exceedingly abundantly above all that we ask or think, according to the power that worketh in us. (Ephesians 3:20 KJV)

Throat Chakra Affirmation

I communicate effectively with everyone in my life. I am calm, confident, and well-spoken. I express my feelings easily and freely.

Let the words of my mouth, and the meditation of my heart, be acceptable in thy sight, O Lord, my strength, and my redeemer. (Psalm 19:14 KJV)

Heart Chakra Affirmation

My emotions are balanced and in harmony with my energy. I love myself in every area of my life. I give love, and love comes back to me.

But above all these things
put on love, which is
the bond of perfection.
(Colossians 3:14 NKJV)

Root Chakra Affirmation

Abundance in this universe is unlimited, and I have the power to receive it.

May the God of hope fill you all with joy and peace as you trust in Him, so that you may overflow with hope by the power of the Holy Spirit. (Romans 15:13 NIV)

Sacral Chakra Affirmation

I forgive my past and embrace all of the present. I am open to receive all that life offers. I have a healthy state of passion and desire in my life.

73

For God so loved the world, that he gave his only son, that whoever believes in him should not perish but have eternal life. (John 3:16 NIV)

Solar Plexus Affirmation

I am a powerful, radiant, and
magnificent being of light.

Let your light so shine before men, that they may see your good works, and glorify your Father which is in heaven. (Matthew 5:16 KJV)

Abundance Affirmation

I release all resistance to money and
allow it to flow joyfully in my life.

The thief does not come except to steal, and to kill, and to destroy. I have come that they may have life, and that they may have it more abundantly. (John 10:10 NKJV)

Prosperity Affirmation

The money I spend enriches
the world and comes back
to me multiplied.

Submit to God and be at peace with him; in this way, prosperity will come to you. (Job 22:21 NIV)

80

Integrity Affirmation

Everything I do is for the higher good of all concerned. Honesty is a value that I honor every day.

Teach me thy way, O Lord;
I will walk in thy truth:
unite my heart to fear thy
name. (Psalm 86:11 KJV)

Forgiveness Affirmation

I forgive those who have wronged
me and choose to live a life full
of love, joy, and peace. I forgive
everyone in my past for all perceived
wrongs and release them into love.

For if ye forgive men their trespasses, your heavenly Father will also forgive you. (Matthew 6:14 KJV)

Love Affirmation

**I am surrounded by love
and prosperity.**

Be strong and take heart,
all you who hope in the
Lord. (Psalm 31:24 NIV)

Inspiration Affirmation

I am the source of love, joy, and
inspiration to myself and others.

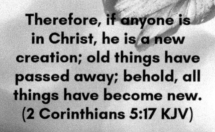

Therefore, if anyone is in Christ, he is a new creation; old things have passed away; behold, all things have become new. (2 Corinthians 5:17 KJV)

Peace Affirmation

**My body feels peaceful energy
flowing in and around me regularly.**

Finally, brothers and sisters, rejoice! Strive for full restoration, encourage one another, be of one mind, live in peace. And the God of love and peace will be with you. (2 Corinthians 13:11 NIV)

Health Affirmation

I am healthy and happy both
physically and mentally.

He that dwelleth in the secret place of the most high shall abide under the shadow of the Almighty. (Psalm 91:1 KJV)

Faith Affirmation

I live by faith, not by sight.
God is with me always. All my
actions, thoughts, and words
are guided by a divine power.

Therefore, I tell you, whatever you ask for in prayer, believe that you have received it, and it will be yours. (Mark 11:24 KJV)

Archangel Michael Protection Prayer

Saint Michael, the archangel, defend us in battle. Be our protection against the wickedness and snares of the devil. May God rebuke him, we humbly pray. And do thou, O prince of the Heavenly Host, by the power of God, thrust into hell Satan and all evil spirits who wander through the world, seeking the ruin of souls. Amen.

For he will command his angels concerning you to guard you in all your ways. (Psalm 91:11 NIV)

Fearlessness Affirmation

I replace fearful thoughts with positive ones.

Casting all your care
upon him; for he careth
for you. (1 Peter 5:7 KJV)

Alignment Affirmation

I am in harmony with my
purpose and manifestation. I
am aligned with greatness.

A man's heart plans his way, But the LORD directs his steps. (Proverbs 16:9 NKJV)

Health Affirmation

My body is balanced and thriving. I have an abundance of energy. I have a strong and healthy body.

Behold, I will bring it health and cure, and I will cure them, and will reveal unto them the abundance of peace and truth. (Jeremiah 33:6 KJV)

Anxiety Relief
Affirmation

All is well. Everything is working
for my highest good. Out of
this situation, only good will
come. I am safe and free.

Fear thou not; for I am with thee: be not dismayed; for I am thy God: I will strengthen thee; yea, I will help thee; yea, I will uphold thee with the right hand of my righteousness. (Isaiah 41:10 KJV)

About the Author

Raluca felt guided to create this book to help others gain a stronger connection to the divine universe and manifest their dreams through daily affirmations and prayer and to know how impactful it can be in others' lives. She spends time every day thanking the universe for allowing this change within her to grow and is grateful for the miracles and blessings she receives. Through daily affirmations, prayer, and meditation, she has been able to completely transform her life. In the short time of reading daily affirmations and prayers, she was able to manifest happiness, love, and abundance. She was able to tap into the infinite source of compassion that everyone has inside them. Opportunities have popped up that she wouldn't have thought of prior to changing her mindset and allowing the divine to work in her life. Raluca is a firm believer of what you put out in the universe comes back to you. If you focus on positive affirmations and visualize your goals, you will succeed because this is what has been reflected out to the universe.

Raluca Boyle is working on a book series that will have a focus on specific areas that the reader would like to work on. Affirmations and prayers on love, health, and abundance will be some of the upcoming books in her series.